God formed you with
His hands...and loves you
with all His heart.
What a blessing He made,
and what a blessing you are.
I'm praying you know this today!

The LORD bless you and keep you.

NUMBERS 6:24 NIV

It is in Him that you live and move
and have your being. As you go through
this day, consider all that is yours
because you are in Christ.

That first moment when God brought life to you, He said "Yes" to who you were and all that you could be. Today I prayed that you know your true worth in His eyes.

I praise You because I am fearfully and wonderfully made; Your works are wonderful, I know that full well.

PSALM 139:14 NIV

When we stop trying to make ourselves worthy, then we find that we actually are worthy because of who God is!

JENNIFER GERELDS

DaySpring

I'm praying you remember today that the Lord loves you, He celebrates you, and He's so glad you're His.

He is a mighty savior. He will take delight in you with gladness. With His love, He will calm all your fears. He will rejoice over you with joyful songs.

ZEPHANIAH 3:17 NLT

Christ was, is, and will always be the quintessential example of what unconditional love looks like.

Susan Goss

No doubt about it, no way around it—God's plan is good, His power is great, and His best is yet to come! I'm praying His wonderful plan for your life will be revealed very soon.

O LORD…Your thoughts toward us cannot be recounted to You in order; if I would declare and speak of them, they are more than can be numbered.

PSALM 40:5 NKJV

You've been praying your heart out, and guess what? God hears every single prayer. He is taking those prayers and turning them into something beautiful.

KATY FULTS

I'm praying your heart will
receive all that the Lord has to give.
He wants the very best for you...and
that's just what He will provide.

When you pass through the waters,
I will be with you; and when you pass through
the rivers, they will not sweep over you.

ISAIAH 43:2 NIV

God speaks in both thunders and whispers,
but in His silence He speaks much more.
Silence is a time for self-reflection, for
listening. Lean into the silence.
Be still with Him.

Linda Kozar

*I'm praying you'll feel God's
presence as He walks each step
with you, holds your hand,
and guides you. His love will be
with you wherever you go.*

The words I speak are not My own,
but My Father who lives in Me does
His work through Me.

JOHN 14:10 NLT

Any time life comes to a halt
and surroundings look foreign...
God has a purpose.

LISA STILWELL

Your life is a reflection of the Father's heart. I'm praying that the Lord will help you carry your light and love wherever you go.

The sweetness of a man's friend gives delight by hearty counsel.

PROVERBS 27:9 NKJV

God wants you to understand your purpose. Everything you've encountered—even the awful things—have been part of your journey.

Marshawn Evans Daniels

You are truly a gift from God.
He chose and created you,
brought you into the world,
and into lives that needed
one-and-only you. Praying you
feel His love for you today.

I always thank my God for you because of
His grace given you in Christ Jesus.
I CORINTHIANS 1:4 NIV

But the One who made this earth knows
you from the inside out . . . delights in your
particular laugh . . . and hears exactly
what you're saying with your heart.

SHANNA NOEL

I pray you always remember that God is for you. He loves you. He believes in you. He won't fail you. He'll be with you. He'll provide for you. He'll bless you. He'll give you rest. He'll strengthen you. Always.

May the LORD bless you and protect you. May the LORD smile on you and be gracious to you. May the LORD show you His favor and give you His peace.

NUMBERS 6:24–26 NLT

Let every horizon remind you of this: Where you see limits, God sees possibility.

Shanna Noel

*I'm praying God will show
you the beauty of His freedom.
His love is deep and wide—
so that you can live a full life
of overflowing joy!*

For there is born to you this day in the city of
David a Savior, who is Christ the Lord.

LUKE 2:11 NKJV

Fear of retribution and punishment keeps
us from looking at and confessing our
indiscretions, but Jesus responds just the
opposite when we do—He holds His arms
wide and calls us by name.

LISA STILWELL

God knows our greatest needs, and He delights in fulfilling them. I'm praying you not only see all your needs met by Him today but that you sense His desire to delight your heart as well.

The Spirit you received brought about your adoption to sonship. And by Him we cry, "Abba, Father."

ROMANS 8:15 NIV

When we feel out of control and are unsure of what is next, we can take great comfort in the fact that our God is always fighting for our best and preparing the way to get there.

Cleere Cherry

We can't be certain of what tomorrow will bring, but we can be certain of God's love. Praying the power of that love fills your life today.

For the Mighty One is holy,
and He has done great things for me.

LUKE 1:49 NLT

God isn't afraid of the dark.
In the beginning He spoke life-words
into it and said, "Let there be light."

HOLLEY GERTH

Chances are, more people than you realize notice God's love through you. Thank you for making a difference in your world. I'm praying you see the impact you have and feel blessed in return.

Let, I pray, Your merciful kindness be for my comfort, according to Your word to Your servant.

PSALM 119:76 NKJV

Truth is the light of God that overcomes the darkness of every lie that seeks to rob you of your peace, steal your joy, and quench your faith.

Roy Lessin

*I'm asking God to bless you
with everlasting joy. May He
keep you safe in your goings and
comings. May He bring many
special things into your life.*

We who have fled to take hold
of the hope set before us may be
greatly encouraged. We have this hope as
an anchor for the soul, firm and secure.
HEBREWS 6:18–19 NIV

*With unlimited resources and riches, God
stands ready to supply all that you need.*

JENNIFER GERELDS

The Lord designed every detail of who you are. He cares about you so much. I'm asking Him to highlight ways that you have been designed to impact the world around you.

Then God looked over all He had made, and He saw that it was very good!

GENESIS 1:31 NLT

As we fix our eyes on God and stop comparing ourselves with others, we lose the pressure of conforming. Then we can encourage and celebrate each other without compromising ourselves.

Shanna Noel

Wonderfully made. Gifted. Chosen. Loved. Beautiful. Accepted. Valued. That's who you truly are! I'm praying you'll feel encouraged today, knowing that you are very special and loved.

I will praise You, for I am fearfully and wonderfully made; marvelous are Your works, and that my soul knows very well.

PSALM 139:14 NKJV

The more we look through a lens of gratitude, the more reasons we will find to smile.

SHANNA NOEL

I'm stopping right now,
in the middle of this day, to pray
peace over your overwhelming
moments...and thank the Lord for
His peace. Your storm is big—
but God is so much bigger.

Peace I leave with you; My peace I give you.
I do not give to you as the world gives.
Do not let your hearts be troubled and
do not be afraid.

JOHN 14:27 NIV

It may not feel like it, you may not
recognize Him, but God is there.
Now ask Him to stay. Keep engaging
Him in the details of your life,
and know that He hears and He cares.

Lisa Stilwell

In all the world, there is only one you—you have a laugh, a smile, a heart that no one else can duplicate or replace. Your life is a wonderful reason to thank God— which I am doing right now!

You formed me with Your hands;
You made me.

JOB 10:8 NLT

You are a new creation, His special treasure.
You are chosen for greatness.

APRIL RODGERS

I'm praying that God will reveal His perfect plans to you. I have no doubt that as you seek Him, you'll find Him. As promised.

The LORD will perfect that which concerns me;
Your mercy, O LORD, endures forever; do not
forsake the works of Your hands.

PSALM 138:8 NKJV

Jesus is the name to call on for deliverance—
through not just some but all trouble.

Lisa Stilwell

DaySpring

I'm praying you'll see God's special purpose for your life— not just for today but for every day of your life.

Do not fear, for I have redeemed you; I have summoned you by name; you are Mine.

ISAIAH 43:1 NIV

Jesus had the chance to be the most popular person in Israel. But becoming a fish-and-loaves factory wasn't why Jesus was sent. He had his eyes fixed on the cross, the tomb, and eternal life with us.

HOLLEY GERTH

Just think... God has allowed you to be here at this time in history to fulfill His special purpose for this generation. I'm asking Him to show you His purposes and give you everything you need to accomplish them.

I cry out to God Most High, to God who will fulfill His purpose for me.

PSALM 57:2 NLT

You are the perfect vessel for God's work, and you can be confident that you make a bright difference in the world around you.

Trieste Vaillancourt

DaySpring

The Lord's care for you is greater than any understanding. I believe He has purposed you for something truly special—and I will pray that you keep Him in your sight as He leads you to it.

The LORD will guide you continually,
and satisfy your soul in drought,
and strengthen your bones.

ISAIAH 58:11 NKJV

Faith and hope begin afresh with each new day. So keep looking. Keep standing. Keep believing in the One who brings the victory for us. He is with you.

LISA STILWELL

Today I'm praying you'll feel God's closeness and know how much He truly cares for you.

The eternal God is your refuge, and underneath are the everlasting arms. He will drive out your enemies before you, saying, 'Destroy them!'

DEUTERONOMY 33:27 NIV

People walk around hiding their private pain, alone and despairing. But we have a God who sees past our walls, deep into our hearts where we hurt the most, and He cares.

Jennifer Gerelds

DaySpring

God sees you are hurting—
He sees your pain and feels your
grief. I'm praying that He will
bring you comfort, peace,
and hope today.

You have collected all my tears
in Your bottle. You have recorded
each one in Your book.

PSALM 56:8 NLT

No matter what happened yesterday, God
promises that we don't have to dwell on the
bruises, battle scars, or regrets of the past.

CLEERE CHERRY REAVES

DaySpring

I prayed for God to sit next to you, put His arms around you, listen to every word, and hold you tightly through your tears. Can you feel His presence?

The LORD is near to all who call upon Him,
to all who call upon Him in truth.

PSALM 145:18 NKJV

God doesn't abandon us the way imperfect
people and unpredictable circumstances do.

Marshawn Evans Daniels

At times it's hard to see which decision to make or path to take. I'm asking the Lord to guide you in a way that others see your peace and trust in Him.

Even though I walk through the darkest valley,
I will fear no evil, for You are with me;
Your rod and Your staff, they comfort me.

PSALM 23:4 NIV

God continues to use us, love us, claim us, and fight for us. His forgiveness is strong and all-encompassing. Nothing overpowers it.

CLEERE CHERRY REAVES

DaySpring

The answers aren't always easy, and the direction is not always clear. I'm praying God will give you the hope and strength to put your life into His very capable hands.

My future is in Your hands.

PSALM 31:15 NLT

There will never be a situation, conversation, or circumstance when God is not with us and working on our behalf.

Holley Gerth

I'm praying for you to know the wisdom of God's ways, the goodness of His love, and the assurance of His presence as He keeps you close every step of the way.

The steps of a good man are ordered by the LORD, and He delights in his way.

PSALM 37:23 NKJV

There's no ocean so wide that God can't cross it to reach you. No desert so dry that He can't rain down His love and mercy. God will stop at nothing to love you.

TRIESTE VAILLANCOURT

I pray that when you walk,
the Lord will guide you.
That when you run, He will sustain
you. That when you fly—yes, when
you fly—that He will take you
places you never dreamed.

Those who hope in the LORD will renew
their strength. They will soar on wings like
eagles; they will run and not grow weary,
they will walk and not be faint.

ISAIAH 40:31 NIV

You don't need to stay stuck in your fears,
afraid of what is to come, wondering
who can help. God is a shield and
source of comfort like no other.

Jennifer Gerelds

You're so strong and brave and beautiful. Not everyone can do what you do. Not everyone can handle things the way you can. So I'm asking God to strengthen you and give you all you need... today and every day.

So be strong and courageous,
all you who put your hope in the LORD!

PSALM 31:24 NLT

God loves you and has only your good—
and His glory—in mind.

LISA STILWELL

No force on earth is more
powerful or effective than
the power of prayer.
And I'm praying for you!

Call to Me, and I will answer you, and show you
great and mighty things, which you do not know.

JEREMIAH 33:3 NKJV

Where we place our focus determines our
level of peace in the present moment.

Jennifer Gerelds

I prayed that God would give you a bright outlook on life as you take the first steps in accomplishing your wildest dreams.

Hope in God, who richly provides us with everything for our enjoyment.

I TIMOTHY 6:17 NIV

God's grace is enough to keep you on your feet and lead you toward your holy purpose.

LISA STILWELL

I asked God to open your eyes to the true blessing of being His child, and to help you live your life in a way that celebrates being blessed, chosen, and created by the Kings of kings.

I will bless you...and you will be a blessing to others.

GENESIS 12:2 NLT

Our today does not have to be the story of our tomorrow, and our potential is not determined by our past. Gulp in that fresh air. It is good to be alive when Jesus is our King.

Cleere Cherry Reaves

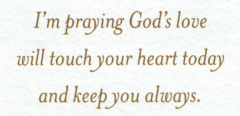

I'm praying God's love
will touch your heart today
and keep you always.

Oh, taste and see that the LORD is good;
blessed is the man who trusts in Him!

PSALM 34:8 NKJV

The focus of the God of the universe is on
you individually, and He loves you beyond
anything that you can do or imagine.

APRIL RODGERS

My prayer for you today is that God gives you peace, hope, and understanding, and He equips you with everything you need to face whatever lies ahead.

He who did not spare His own Son, but gave Him up for us all—how will He not also, along with Him, graciously give us all things?

ROMANS 8:32 NIV

When the world around us tries to tell us who we are, let's pause and listen for the only voice that gets the final say.

Holley Gerth

I'm praying that the Great Physician—the One who made you and knows how to mend you—would restore your body, soul, and spirit. His schedule is never full. His diagnosis is always accurate. His treatment is wise…and His results—amazing!

Healthy people don't need a doctor—
sick people do. I have come to call not those
who think they are righteous, but those
who know they are sinners.

MARK 2:17 NLT

*Waiting on God's plan
is always worth it.*

KATY FULTS

I prayed for Jesus to remind you that you never have to face anything alone. May you live today with confidence that you CAN overcome!

In Him we live and move and have our being.

ACTS 17:28 NKJV

What God has already done in your life, He will continue to do. God will continue to make you an overcomer. He will continue to help you persevere.

Holley Gerth

I'm praying that you know deep in your heart that God will protect you, comfort you, and give you peace. He will listen to you, strengthen you, and carry you. Because He loves you so much.

I have loved you with an everlasting love;
I have drawn you with unfailing kindness.

JEREMIAH 31:3 NIV

When we approach the people and circumstances of life confident in who God created us specifically to be, we usher breathtaking beauty and perspective into this world.

JENNIFER GERELDS

In the ever-changing circumstances of life, there is a faithful, never-changing God in control. Every day begins and ends with His purpose, and I've asked Him to lead you with His strength and love along the way.

All the believers lifted their voices together in prayer to God: "O Sovereign Lord, Creator of heaven and earth, the sea, and everything in them...."

ACTS 4:24 NLT

God's presence is before us;
His voice calls us to Himself and
where He wants us to go—places filled with
love, forgiveness, power, and healing.
Our living hope lies in Christ,
not in our past.

Lisa Stilwell

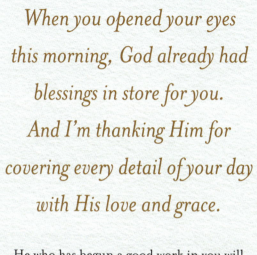

When you opened your eyes
this morning, God already had
blessings in store for you.
And I'm thanking Him for
covering every detail of your day
with His love and grace.

He who has begun a good work in you will
complete it until the day of Jesus Christ.

PHILIPPIANS 1:6 NKJV

By yourself, it's impossible.
But with God, all things are possible.

SHANNA NOEL

Today, I prayed you would be reminded of three things: You are stronger than you ever imagined. Jesus is closer than you ever realized. You are loved more than you ever knew.

I hear about your love for all His holy people and your faith in the Lord Jesus.

PHILEMON 1:5 NIV

New life begins to grow where old wounds once were. God seals those places with His grace, healing you by His love and freeing you to face whatever may come your way today.

Jennifer Gerelds

DaySpring

I'm asking God to stay close to you on your journey, giving you wisdom and peace, with His perfect love along the way.

I will never leave you nor forsake you.

HEBREWS 13:5 NKJV

He's not looking for your accomplishments; He's looking for your availability.

MARSHAWN EVANS DANIELS

I asked God to remind you

that you're never, ever alone.

Nothing takes Him by surprise.

He is the God of new beginnings.

And His love never, ever gives up.

My grace is all you need.
My power works best in weakness.

II CORINTHIANS 12:9 NLT

The One who created your body to
self-heal packs a supernatural power to restore
your soul. As you allow God's love to wrap
around your hurt, a miracle will happen.

Jennifer Gerelds

God is with us always, but in the times we are deeply hurting, we often need to feel His presence even more strongly. And He promises His presence. I'm praying you feel Him today.

May the God of hope fill you with all joy and peace as you trust in Him.

ROMANS 15:13 NIV

As long as we fix our eyes and hearts and minds on Jesus, we can't look back. His presence is before us; His voice calls us to Himself and where He wants us to go.

LISA STILWELL

DaySpring

God created every detail of you. He knows you better and loves you more than anyone. He's your wise Father and faithful friend, who takes great joy in you. I'm praying that the reality of these truths overwhelms you today!

How precious also are Your thoughts to me, O God! How great is the sum of them!

PSALM 139:17 NKJV

Your struggles are connected to your calling and are, in part, what qualify you for greater impact.

Marshawn Evans Daniels

You are a gift from God
in the lives of so many people
who have been blessed to know
you. Thank you for being your
authentic self. I'm asking God to
delight your heart in the way you
have done for so many.

You have a special place in my heart.
PHILIPPIANS 1:7 NLT

As God's child, there is nothing
in the truth of God to depress you,
defeat you, discourage you, or deflate
you. The truth will build you up,
lift you up, and keep you up.

ROY LESSIN

When we struggle to know ourselves, we can rest in the fact that God knows us fully. When we are misunderstood, God knows and understands us. May you find joy in the God who loves you more than you know.

Never will I leave you; never will I forsake you.

HEBREWS 13:5 NIV

It's easy to feel as if our imperfections disqualify us from being used by God in a mighty way, but let's not forget that Jesus hand-selected everyday people to be His disciples.

Marshawn Evans Daniels

Thanking God today for the gift of you and asking Him to lift you up and strengthen you in every way.

He raises the poor from the dust
and lifts the beggar from the ash heap,
to set them among princes and make them
inherit the throne of glory.

I SAMUEL 2:8 NKJV

The water Jesus gives is "living water" (John 4:10); it's not of this world. It comes from God's own Spirit, filling every child of God.

JENNIFER GERELDS

I'm thanking God for all the ways He shines His love through you!

The Spirit...makes you holy and through your belief in the truth.

II THESSALONIANS 2:13 NLT

Grace abounds to you today with
so many favors, blessings, and joys.

Roy Lessin

Each and every day is a
gift from God, lovingly
prepared, covered with His grace,
and wrapped with the quiet
strength your heart will need.
I pray you know how much
He delights in you!

You are precious and honored
in My sight, and...I love you.

ISAIAH 43:4 NIV

We may not know what is
ahead of us, but we can be absolutely
certain of Who is with us.

HOLLEY GERTH

I'm asking God to stay

extra close to you today.

*Behold, the virgin shall be with child, and bear a
Son, and they shall call His name "Immanuel,"
which is translated, "God with us."*

MATTHEW 1:23 NKJV

Nothing catches God by surprise, nothing
is too difficult for God to navigate,
and nothing is bigger than God.

Marshawn Evans Daniels

DaySpring

Today, I prayed for you
to feel the depth of
God's love for you.

For all of God's promises have been
fulfilled in Christ with a resounding "Yes!"
II CORINTHIANS 1:20 NLT

The invitation to drink from God's
refreshing and replenishing store of love
and hope is with us every single day.

JENNIFER GERELDS

You aren't what other people say about you, condemned for making a mistake or shamed before you're forgiven. I pray you have the strength to believe—you are priceless, loved, whole, the joy of God's heart.

All have sinned and fall short of the glory of God, and all are justified freely by His grace through the redemption that came by Christ Jesus.

ROMANS 3:23–24 NIV

Christ is the cleansing and refreshing relief that humankind has been waiting for.

Anita Higman

You are irreplaceable.
You are chosen. You are
treasured. You truly are as
beautiful as God sees you!
I'm praying you'll fully
grasp these truths today.

Blessed be the God and Father of
our Lord Jesus Christ, who has blessed
us with every spiritual blessing in the
heavenly places in Christ.

EPHESIANS 1:3 NKJV

God loved us before the earth was even created.
He knew that we would be right where we are,
shining His light and living as His beloved
before this big, crazy world even existed.

APRIL RODGERS

DaySpring

You're very much loved and valued, not only by those who know you, but by the One who created you. God and I are both celebrating your life—because you are truly one of a kind!

God will rejoice over you as a bridegroom rejoices over his bride.

ISAIAH 62:5 NLT

If you're putting pressure on yourself today to do more, be more, or achieve more, then pause and take a deep breath. Just be faithful.

Holley Gerth

You have a laugh, a smile,
a heart that no one else can
duplicate or replace.
You're God's design, and I'm
asking Him to show you exactly
how wonderfully unique you are!

In Him we were also chosen...according to
the plan of Him who works out everything in
conformity with the purpose of His will.

EPHESIANS 1:11 NIV

What worries you today? Your Father knows
... and He will fully satisfy the deepest
needs of your body and soul.

JENNIFER GERELDS

It may not always feel like it, but you're making a difference, living your life, quietly serving and doing what needs to be done. Whether you hear it or not, others—including me—are thanking God for you.

For in Christ Jesus neither circumcision nor uncircumcision avails anything, but faith working through love.

GALATIANS 5:6 NKJV

We matter to Him. Let's ask Him to open our blind eyes and believe His promises.

Jennifer Gerelds

When we pour all we
have into God's hands, He sifts
it like sand, uncovering gems
and letting our lives reflect the
sparkling beauty of His grace.
Your gifts are a gift to many,
and I'm thanking Him for that.

We also pray that you will be strengthened
with all his glorious power so you will have
all the endurance and patience you need.
May you be filled with joy.

COLOSSIANS 1:11 NLT

We're God's workmanship,
not His minions. We're kind of like
specially made locks, and He possesses the
one-of-a-kind key to each of us.

SHANNA NOEL

God has a path for your
feet to follow, a plan for your
heart to discover, and a purpose
for your life to fulfill. I'm asking
Him to guide your steps with
wisdom and courage.

Your love, LORD, endures forever—
do not abandon the works of Your hands.

PSALM 138:8 NIV

You are the carrier of a unique message
from heaven that only your life
experiences and abilities can convey.

Marshawn Evans Daniels

Not a moment of our lives is out of God's control. Today I pray that you'll see many reminders of how special you are to Him... and how close He is to you.

You discern my going out and my lying down;
You are familiar with all my ways.

PSALM 139:3 NIV

God's Word doesn't advise us to control our outward circumstances so we can produce a desired feeling. We're pointed inwardly first—to choose the attitude of our hearts no matter what.

CLEERE CHERRY REAVES

God holds the ones who are hurting. I'm praying you feel His arms around you as He tenderly holds you, lovingly comforts you, and faithfully walks with you every step of your life.

He shall cover you with His feathers, and under His wings you shall take refuge.

PSALM 91:4 NKJV

We're always invited to give the gift of forgiveness. We've surely received it ourselves, and the more we practice giving it, the freer we will be.

Shanna Noel

DaySpring

When your heart trembles, I'm praying He's near, to bring every comfort and catch every tear. His comfort is gentle, His whispered words, true. His love is the balm that will carry you through.

You prepare a table before me in the presence of my enemies. You anoint my head with oil; my cup overflows.

Psalm 23:5 NIV

God does, in fact, prepare tables of delight right in front of our enemies, and He invites us to come and sit in the comfort of His company—no matter what mayhem swirls around us.

JENNIFER GERELDS

Today, I prayed for you to feel God's presence like never before.

All things work together for good to those who love God, to those who are the called according to His purpose.

ROMANS 8:28 NKJV

It's okay if we can't feel, see, or even fully understand what God says is true of us yet. What matters is that we don't trust our human identity to be our ultimate destiny.

Holley Gerth

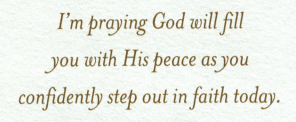

*I'm praying God will fill
you with His peace as you
confidently step out in faith today.*

What is our lot from God above,
our heritage from the Almighty on high?…
Does He not see my ways and
count my every step?

JOB 31:2-4 NIV

*We are not left alone to fight
for a better day. The Lord hears
when we call His name.*

LISA STILWELL

DaySpring

I know you don't feel like everything is under control, but God's got you! I prayed He would take away your stress and anxiety today and replace it with the assurance that He is taking care of all of it— every single detail.

Through the LORD's mercies we are not consumed, because His compassions fail not. They are new every morning; great is Your faithfulness.

LAMENTATIONS 3:22–23 NKJV

Jesus can shine the lightest light into the darkest dark.

Trieste Vaillancourt

*I'm praying you feel safe
in God's loving arms today.
When you can't, He can.*

All glory to God, who is able,
through His mighty power at work
within us, to accomplish infinitely
more than we might ask or think.

EPHESIANS 3:20 NLT

*Jesus is the name to call for the strength to
endure. For the faith to keep going. And to
fan the flame of hope and keep it burning.*

LISA STILWELL

As you step out today,

know that you're prayed

for—and very loved.

Those He predestined, He also called;
those He called, He also justified;
those He justified, He also glorified.

ROMANS 8:30 NIV

Your job is not to produce light,
it is simply to shine God's light.
You just be you, and He will do the rest.

April Rodgers

*I'm asking God to release you
from all fear and to instead fill
you with His love—a love that
covers and guards you completely.*

The LORD will command His lovingkindness in
the daytime, and in the night His song shall be
with me—a prayer to the God of my life.

PSALM 42:8 NKJV

*If you are in need of comfort today,
God will comfort you, and the comfort
you receive today will help you comfort
someone in need tomorrow.*

ROY LESSIN

*Asking God to fill
you with joy, peace,
purpose, love, and hope.*

Whatever is good and perfect is a
gift coming down to us from God our
Father, who created all the lights in the heavens.
He never changes or casts a shifting shadow.

JAMES 1:17 NLT

God has all power at His fingertips.
But it's you He wants above all else.

Trieste Vaillancourt

I'm praying God will help you walk in true realization of His unfailing, unconditional love for you.

Do not fear, for I have redeemed you; I have summoned you by name; you are Mine.

ISAIAH 43:1 NIV

When we approach the people and circumstances of life confident in who God created us specifically to be, we usher breathtaking beauty and perspective into this world.

JENNIFER GERELDS

*I'm praying you'll see
God's blessings unfold right
in front of you today.*

*I thank my God always concerning
you for the grace of God which was
given to you by Christ Jesus.*

I CORINTHIANS 1:4 NKJV

God is going to show up.
That is assured.
The rest of the details?
They really are somewhat irrelevant.

Cleere Cherry Reaves

God's power is limitless,
His character changeless, and
His love endless! I'm praying you
know, without a doubt, that no
matter what you are facing,
He is with you.

Don't be afraid!…I bring you good news that
will bring great joy to all people.

LUKE 2:10 NLT

God isn't afraid of the dark, and we
don't have to be either. Even when we
can't feel Him through the longest
nights—He is always there.

HOLLEY GERTH

I'm asking God to strengthen your heart and give you an everlasting hope.

You make known to me the path of life;
You will fill me with joy in Your presence,
with eternal pleasures at Your right hand.

PSALM 16:11 NIV

When we choose to let go of what
we're holding onto and instead trust in the
Lord with every ounce of our hearts,
He will give us the strength to walk in His way,
even if it looks different than our own.

Katy Fults

I'm praying that God's love for you would be like a compass— guiding your heart and your steps into all that is best.

And this is eternal life, that they may
know You, the only true God,
and Jesus Christ whom You have sent.

JOHN 17:3 NKJV

If your life is in a place that's nothing like what you planned, God has a purpose. It can actually be the beginning of one of the richest times you've ever experienced.

LISA STILWELL

There's no love that's greater—
or more wonderful, more wild,
more passionate, more powerful—
than the love of Jesus. May that
love overtake and overwhelm you
today, in every way.

There is no God like You in all of heaven and
earth. You keep Your covenant and show
unfailing love to all who walk before You in
wholehearted devotion.

II CHRONICLES 6:14 NLT

The love of God in you first comes
to bless and enrich your life,
but its course is to flow out from
within you to touch and
enrich other hearts.

Roy Lessin

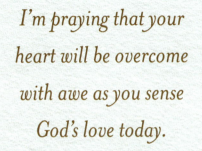

I'm praying that your heart will be overcome with awe as you sense God's love today.

She will give birth to a son, and you are to give Him the name Jesus, because He will save His people from their sins.

MATTHEW 1:21 NIV

Our loving God not only supplies but also multiplies. He will give us everything we need to do His will.

HOLLEY GERTH

I pray God's care is close to you and that His kindness covers you like raindrops from above.

Casting all your care upon Him, for He cares for you.

I PETER 5:7 NKJV

God is walking your path with you now. He hears every word that spills from your mouth and feels your heartache or struggle or whatever it is you're going through.

Lisa Stilwell

Today I asked God to do what only He can—strengthen you with His love, fill you with His assurance, bless you with His peace, and hold you in His arms.

For the LORD your God…will take delight in you with gladness. With His love, He will calm all your fears. He will rejoice over you with joyful songs.

ZEPHANIAH 3:17 NLT

We may never know why some things happen, but we can always know Who is with us—to help and to heal and sometimes just to be. He is our love, and he cares.

LISA STILWELL

Sometimes life just doesn't make any sense. But even in those moments, some things remain true—God loves us so well. He has a perfect plan. He never leaves. I'm praying you feel the comfort of all His promises.

No one will be able to stand against you all the days of your life...I will never leave you nor forsake you.

JOSHUA 1:5 NIV

If you're striving for perfection and trying to make everyone happy, let go of those unrealistic expectations. Just be faithful.

Holley Gerth

*Praying that when you need
it most, you'll see God extend
His hand to hold, help, and guide
you. You never have to feel
alone because He's always
walking close beside you.*

Though I walk through the valley of the shadow
of death, I will fear no evil; for You are with
me; Your rod and Your staff, they comfort me.

PSALM 23:4 NKJV

*Nothing surprises God because He knows
the past, present, and future. He can't be
derailed or disappointed. He doesn't grow
weary. He doesn't give up, give in, or let go.*

HOLLEY GERTH

I prayed that God would place people in your life who will demonstrate His love for you in wonderful ways.

I thank God for you…Night and day I constantly remember you in my prayers.

II TIMOTHY 1:3 NLT

Each of us offers a unique perspective, a delightfully different personality through which the love and grace of God can flow.

Jennifer Gerelds

I'm asking God to guide
you today, giving you
the wisdom and strength to
face every decision ahead of you
with confidence and courage.

Before I formed you in the womb I knew you,
before you were born I set you apart.

JEREMIAH 1:5 NIV

You don't have be "good enough"
or even try to figure it all out. Just go,
and God will take care of the rest.

JENNIFER GERELDS

I'm praying God will
free you from any unrealistic
expectations you've placed on
yourself and that you will sense
His calming power today.

*Come to Me, all you who labor and are heavy
laden, and I will give you rest.*

MATTHEW 11:28 NKJV

When confronted with options, we can ask,
"What's God's best in my life today?"
We discover the answer by spending
time in His presence with His
Word and by listening to His heart.

Holley Gerth

Asking God to open your eyes to the extraordinary today!

The Spirit of God, who raised
Jesus from the dead, lives in you.

ROMANS 8:11 NLT

When we pray to the God of the universe
for things that seem impossible and
unrealistic, it is the perfect opportunity
for him to make miracles happen.

CLEERE CHERRY REAVES

Jesus is altogether mighty, altogether lovely, and altogether good. I'm praying that Jesus is real in your circumstances today.

*Here I am! I stand at the door and knock.
If anyone hears My voice and opens the door,
I will come in and eat with that person,
and they with Me.*

REVELATION 3:20 NIV

You don't need to stay stuck in your fears, afraid of what is to come, wondering who can help. Leave the isolation of self-reliance and turn to God Almighty.

Jennifer Gerelds

God's love is more life-changing than any of us realize. I'm asking Him to show Himself at work in a way that puts you in awe of Him and His love.

For God so loved the world that He gave His only begotten Son, that whoever believes in Him should not perish but have everlasting life.

JOHN 3:16 NKJV

God has invited us to taste and see just how good He is. It's written all through His Word, and it shines all through His world.

JENNIFER GERELDS

I'm praying God's
love will heal
your wounded heart.

"Come now, let's settle this," says the LORD.
"Though your sins are like scarlet,
I will make them as white as snow."

ISAIAH 1:18 NLT

If we allow ourselves to grieve
properly and hold fast to our Savior,
before long we'll find that we are able
to praise Him even through the pain.

April Rodgers

What does God think of you? Unique. Gifted. Accepted. Enjoyed. Embraced. Loved. His special recipe included all the good stuff! It can be hard to believe you're that special… but I'm praying you can believe it today.

God created mankind in His own image, in the image of God He created them; male and female He created them.

GENESIS 1:27 NIV

No one on this earth knows you as well as God does.

SHANNA NOEL

I'm asking God to show you some of the ways you make a difference every day. God made you special, and you can't help but shine wherever you go.

I have not stopped giving thanks for you, remembering you in my prayers.

EPHESIANS 1:16 NIV

God repairs broken wings, speaks life into souls, and reminds weary hearts that our feet were never meant to stay on the ground.

Cleere Cherry Reaves

*As you go about
your day, I'm praying
that God will reveal
Himself to you in amazing ways!*

I am the LORD your God,
who rescued you.

EXODUS 20:2 NLT

*God is a shield and source of comfort like no
other. Not only is He right beside us, He is
above us, below us, before us, and behind us!*

JENNIFER GERELDS

As hard as it can be,
I'm praying that you will be
courageous in that thing
God is calling you to do. Tip:
Don't wait to "feel" courageous.
Just act as if you already are.

Be strong and courageous, and do
the work. Do not be afraid or discouraged,
for the LORD God, my God, is with you.

I CHRONICLES 28:20 NIV

God sees every detail of our lives.
He's been with us in every
step we've ever taken.

Holley Gerth

God uses imperfect people
with impossible dreams to do
incredible, God-sized things.
I'm praying for big things for you!

He has shown you, O man, what is good;
and what does the LORD require of you
but to do justly, to love mercy, and to
walk humbly with your God?

MICAH 6:8 NKJV

You've been praying your heart out, and
guess what? God hears every single prayer.
He is taking those prayers and turning
them into something beautiful.

KATY FULTS

I'm praying that God will reveal His great plans for you today. I know He is working in your life and a door will open soon.

When you go through deep waters,
I will be with you…When you walk through
the fire of oppression, you will not be burned up;
the flames will not consume you.

ISAIAH 43:2 NLT

It's in the trials and hurdles
where we not only rise to more
than we ever thought possible,
but also to where we create
new stages for highlighting
His glory.

Lisa Stilwell

I'm praying God will fill you with His peace and joy today.

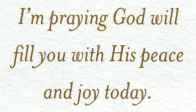

She gave this name to the LORD who spoke to her: "You are the God who sees me," for she said, "I have now seen the One who sees me."

GENESIS 16:13 NIV

Jesus exudes love because He is love! Jesus is our go-to model when we are struggling—because while we were sinners, He died for us (Romans 5:8).

SUSAN GOSS

There's no way to fully understand the pain someone is going through or how deeply they hurt. But there's one certain thing: God's love surrounds, strengthens, and carries. I pray that you feel it today.

For I am persuaded that neither...
height nor depth, nor any other created thing,
shall be able to separate us from the love of
God which is in Christ Jesus our Lord.

ROMANS 8:38–39 NKJV

Jesus wraps His arms around
us and heals our broken hearts.

April Rodgers

I'm praying that God will give you the power, strength, and courage to do the next right thing. I know He will be with you every step of the way.

May He give you the power to accomplish all the good things your faith prompts you to do.

II THESSALONIANS 1:11 NLT

Your life matters to God, and it always will.

APRIL RODGERS

I pray that God's joy will fill your heart every day, every hour, every minute of your life.

*You will show me the way of life,
granting me the joy of Your presence and
the pleasures of living with You forever.*

PSALM 16:11 NLT

Jesus holds His arms wide and calls us
by name. He waits to embrace us with
such love that we're able to
stand in His presence.

Lisa Stilwell

I asked God to help you
move through this day with
a quiet heart, a peaceful
certainty that your life is in
His hands, and a deep trust
in His plan and purposes.

If we live in the Spirit,
let us also walk in the Spirit.

GALATIANS 5:25 NKJV

Without His grace we were stumbling
around, trying to find our purpose.
By His grace we daily walk in the good
things that He has prepared for us.

ROY LESSIN

The God who spoke the world into being, who split the Red Sea, who raised Jesus from the dead, is the same God living in every person belonging to Him. I'm praying His power works mightily in you today.

We are more than conquerors through Him who loved us.

ROMANS 8:37 NKJV

God is love, and God's love is the best kind of love you can have in your heart.

Roy Lessin

God loves you and values you. I prayed you would fully understand how truly amazing you are—and how beautiful you are in His eyes.

Christ will make His home in your hearts as you trust in Him. Your roots will grow down into God's love and keep you strong.

EPHESIANS 3:17 NLT

We can't begin to understand what paths God has for us, but when we let go of the grip on our own plan, we set our hearts free to allow God to guide us.

KATY FULTS